A Character Building Book™

Learning About Dignity from the Life of
Martin Luther King, Jr.

Jeanne Strazzabosco

The Rosen Publishing Group's
PowerKids Press™
New York

Published in 1996 by The Rosen Publishing Group, Inc.
29 East 21st Street, New York, NY 10010

First Edition

Book design: Erin McKenna

Photo credits: Cover © Archive Photos; pp. 4, 8 © Research Photogs/FPG International; all other photos © AP/Wide World Photos.

Strazzabosco, Jeanne.
      Learning about dignity from the life of Martin Luther King, Jr. / Jeanne Strazzabosco.
          p.   cm. — (A character building book)
      Includes index.
      Summary: A brief biography examining the value of dignity in the life of the Baptist minister and civil rights leader whose philosophy and practice of nonviolent civil disobedience helped African Americans win many battles for equal rights.
      ISBN 0-8239-2415-7
      1. King, Martin Luther, Jr., 1929–1968—Juvenile literature. 2. Afro-Americans—Biography—Juvenile literature. 3. Civil rights workers—United States—Biography—Juvenile literature. 4. Baptists—United States—Clergy—Biography—Juvenile literature. 5. Dignity—Juvenile literature. [1. King, Martin Luther, Jr. 1929–1968. 2. Clergy. 3. Civil rights workers. 4. Afro-Americans—Biography. 5. Dignity.] I. Title. II. Series.
E185.97.K5S79 1996
323'.092—dc20   96-20210
                                                                                                                CIP
                                                                                                                 AC

Manufactured in the United States of America

Table of Contents

Martin Luther King, Jr.

Martin Luther King, Jr., was born in Atlanta, Georgia, in 1929. His father was the pastor of a Baptist Church. The Kings lived a good life. But they were faced with anger and **racism** (RAY-sih-zum) every day. They were African American. At that time in the United States, many white people wrongly believed that they were better than blacks. But Martin knew that all people are **equal** (EE-kwul). He believed in his own **dignity** (DIG-nih-tee), and the dignity of all African Americans. He spent most of his life fighting for equal rights for African Americans.

◀ *Martin fought hard for equal rights for African Americans.*

Segregation

Segregation (seh-greh-GAY-shun) kept blacks and whites apart. Black children went to different schools than white children. There were separate restrooms and drinking fountains. Blacks had to sit in the back of buses. They had to sit in the balcony seats at movies, away from the whites, who sat downstairs. Few restaurants would serve African Americans. In stores, they were either ignored by clerks or watched for fear of shoplifting. Although this was unfair, segregation was **legal** (LEE-gul).

It was once legal to separate people by color. ▶

Hurt and Angry

As a child Martin was aware of the racism that surrounded him. He was hurt and angered by it. Martin's father believed that life would someday be better for them. He believed that white people would change their attitudes toward black people. He taught this to Martin. At church, Martin and his family prayed and sang. They organized activites to help improve living and working conditions for all African Americans.

◀ *Martin and his family believed that all people would one day live together peacefully.*

Touched by Racism

Martin loved school. He enjoyed giving speeches and writing. He won first prize in a contest for an essay he wrote about African Americans and the U.S. **Constitution** (kon-stih-TOO-shun). He and his teacher traveled by bus to receive the prize. On the way home, his joy turned to **frustration** (frus-TRAY-shun). A white man got on the bus. The bus driver told Martin to give up his seat to the white man. At first Martin argued and wouldn't give up his seat. But he finally did.

Many people were angry about the way black people were treated. ▶

Mohandas Gandhi

Martin decided to become a pastor, like his father. At Crozer, a school for pastors, he learned about **Mohandas Gandhi** (moh-HON-dus GON-dee). Gandhi was an Indian lawyer and **activist** (AK-tih-vist) who had governed India. Gandhi believed that love was more powerful than violence. Martin had learned that from his father many years before. Gandhi believed in fighting injustice with peaceful **resistance** (ree-ZIS-tens). Martin started to wonder if this might work for African Americans.

◀ *Mohandas Gandhi believed and taught that love was stronger than hate and violence.*

Changing Times

Martin graduated from Crozer at the top of his class. Then he earned his Ph.D. at Boston University. There he met and married Coretta Scott. She loved Martin and believed in his work. They moved to Alabama, where Martin became pastor of a Baptist Church.

In 1954, the U.S. Supreme Court decided to end segregation in schools. Black and white children began to go to the same schools. Martin knew that this was the beginning of change. It was a step in the direction of equality for blacks and whites.

Martin's wife, Coretta, supported Martin's beliefs and work. ▶

Rosa Parks

In 1955, a black woman named Rosa Parks was arrested in Montgomery, Alabama. She had refused to give up her seat on the bus to a white man. The head of the Montgomery National Association for the Advancement of Colored People (NAACP) contacted Martin. They planned a bus **boycott** (BOY-kot) to support Rosa's action. African Americans agreed to stop using buses until the racist rules changed. The boycott lasted for a year. And it worked. In November 1956, the U.S. Supreme Court ruled that blacks could sit anywhere they wanted on buses.

◀ *Rosa Parks's brave act helped start a major move toward equality for African Americans in the U.S.*

Peaceful Protests

Martin continued to believe that nonviolent protest was the only way to make good changes. He formed a group that encouraged churches to work for the rights of African Americans. He joined students in peaceful protests. Students held **sit-ins** (SIT-inz) in restaurants where African Americans were not served. Often the students were **arrested** (uh-RES-tid). Martin was arrested too. He accepted these arrests with dignity. He believed that it was better to be jailed for breaking an unjust law than to accept it.

Martin organized peaceful protests for equal rights. ▶

The March on Washington

Martin organized many protest marches. In the summer of 1963, Martin organized the March on Washington. People of every race took part. More than 250,000 people marched through Washington, DC, with Martin and listened to him speak. He spoke of his dreams for the U.S. He shared his vision that one day all people would be able to live together in peace. In 1964, Martin Luther King, Jr., was awarded the Nobel Peace Prize. In 1965, U.S. President Lyndon B. Johnson created a law ensuring equal voting rights for all people.

◄ *Martin is remembered by many for his courage, strength, and dignity.*

Dignity and Grace

In April 1968, Martin went to Memphis, Tennessee. He went to help a group of workers who were on **strike** (STRYK). He was shot and killed by someone who was afraid of his ideas. He was only 39 years old. Martin had helped the country understand that all people should be treated equally. Martin was a great leader in a time of change. In 1983, the U.S. Government declared January 15, Martin Luther King, Jr.'s birthday, a national holiday. Throughout his life, Martin Luther King, Jr., chose peaceful resistance. He fought for what he believed was right with dignity and grace.

Glossary

activist (AK-tih-vist) Person who fights for what he or she believes.
arrest (uh-REST) To take to jail.
boycott (BOY-kot) To avoid or not buy something.
Constitution (kon-stih-TOO-shun) Set of rules that the U.S. is run by.
dignity (DIG-nih-tee) Self-respect.
equal (EE-kwul) The same in value.
frustration (frus-TRAY-shun) A feeling of being defeated or of
    uselessness.
legal (LEE-gul) Within the law.
Mohandas Gandhi (moh-HON-dus GON-dee) Teacher of and
    believer in peaceful resistance.
racism (RAY-sih-zum) The wrong belief that one race is better
    than another.
resistance (ree-ZIS-tens) Fighting against something.
segregation (seh-greh-GAY-shun) Separation by race.
sit-in (SIT-in) When a group of people "sit" in a place in protest.
strike (STRYK) When workers refuse to work until their demands
    are met.

Index